table of contents

what is cybersecurity?
A great career option!
pages 4-11

pathways
Choose your path to success.
pages 12-13

types of careers
Cybersecurity offers many types of jobs.
pages 14-17

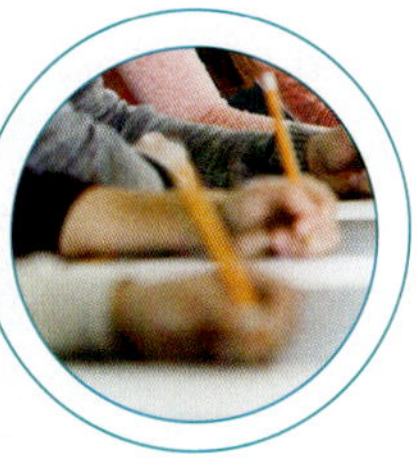

education
High school, community colleges, and universities all offer programs.
pages 18-39

jobs
You can find many opportunities in the government or nearly every company.
pages 40-51

cybersecurity is

A Great Career Option!

Are you into…Computers and video games? Solving puzzles and mysteries? Writing code and programming computers? Tracking criminals? Defending our country? Then, cybersecurity could be for you! Because **CYBERSECURITY IS…**

Defending Our Nation

Cyber criminals, terrorists, and hostile nation states pose serious challenges to maintaining an open and free society — our way of life — in the digital era. Chinese agents stole U.S. government employees' records from the Office of Personnel Management — twice! North Korea successfully penetrated U.S. and South Korean top-secret plans, while Russia interfered in the 2016 presidential election in numerous ways. In addition, national security is affected by criminal assaults on the IT systems of financial institutions and other major businesses too numerous to list. The U.S. response is always evolving and adapting, trying to stay ahead of these threats. In March 2018, for example, the Trump administration imposed sanctions on a series of Russian organizations and individuals in retaliation for interfering in the 2016 elections, as well as other "malicious" cyber attacks. The U.S. Intelligence Community (IC) works across several branches of government to coordinate and execute cybersecurity strategy. The IC is coordinated by the Office of the Director of Intelligence and includes the CIA plus a large group of agencies within the Departments of Defense — such as the U.S Cyber Command — Justice, Homeland Security, and Treasury. It's a real-time, round-the-clock, highest-priority effort.

Safeguarding Telecommunications

Because the telecommunications industry builds, controls, and operates the nation's critical information infrastructure, these businesses are inviting targets for both cyber criminals and foreign adversaries. When Verizon, the largest U.S. mobile phone and Internet service provider, announced that 14 million customers were exposed to a security breach, it was a familiar tale of woe: AT&T and several smaller telecoms had also been attacked. Access to customer data opens the door to individual identity theft and corporate blackmail. In addition to protecting consumers' stored information, telecom companies must protect leased equipment, such as routers, that both individuals and businesses depend on.

Securing Our Money

U.S. banks and investment institutions are potential treasure troves of personal data and money. In recent years, financial services powerhouse JP Morgan Chase had a breach that affected tens of millions of people and seven million businesses. Cyber criminals find holes in software, penetrate information systems, and install their own codes. They target email accounts to steal passwords for bank and credit card accounts (phishing). They also target websites to infect them with malicious software (malware) or programs that lock users out of their own IT systems to force payment for getting sites and systems back (ransomware). And, just recently the U.S. Secret Service warned banks about "jackpotting," a sophisticated crime in which thieves install malicious software and/or hardware at ATMs that force the machines to spit out huge volumes of cash like a Vegas slot machine!

> **CYBERSECURITY FIELD AVERAGE STARTING SALARY:**
> # $75,484*

*WITH SECURITY CLEARANCE & CERTIFICATION. SOURCE: DEPARTMENT OF HOMELAND SECURITY

Protecting Our Electric Grid

Imagine you can't charge your iPhone or get that Xbox up and running. Think of life-support machines in hospitals shut down. That's just what could happen if the U.S. electric power grid comes under a cyber attack. In 2016, one-third of Ukraine's population lost all electricity in a Russian cyber attack. Today's foreign state competitors and adversaries — Iran, North Korea, and China, as well as Russia — are all developing cyber tools to cripple the increasingly computerized and interconnected U.S. electric grid: a shocking possibility.

cybersecurity is

Preserving Our Privacy

Experian, Trans Union, and Equifax, the nation's three largest credit bureaus, hold our most private information: names, Social Security numbers, birthdates, drivers' license numbers, and home addresses. So, when Equifax announced in 2017 that nearly 150 million people in the U.S. had their personal data compromised in more than one hacking incident, consumers were outraged. According to reports, hackers were able to exploit an obvious vulnerability in the Equifax website. Public outrage was a wake-up call: no one can afford to sleep on privacy protection.

Shipping Safely

Talk about roiling the waters! In 2016, A.P. Moeller Maersk, the world's biggest container shipping line and operator of 76 seaports worldwide, was hit by a computer virus that shut down operations across the globe, disrupting normal operations for several weeks. Ports — including Los Angeles, our busiest — were stalled for days, and oil production and transport were affected. The NotPetya virus exploited holes in a Microsoft Windows operating system. Fully 90 percent of the world's trade is transported by sea, and ships that carry that cargo — worth billions — must rely on a GPS navigation system vulnerable to cyber attack. Should the system be more broadly attacked, global shipping could be grounded. The Maersk experience has shipping companies turning back to radio communications for navigation while also steering full steam ahead to better cybersecurity.

WORLDWIDE JOB OPENINGS BY 2019
Over 6 million

Coding Cyber Weapons

In recent years, the U.S as well as foreign adversaries like China, Russia, and North Korea have created increasingly sophisticated tools for conducting online sabotage. The theory behind these weapons is that it allows government intelligence officials the potential to destroy an enemy's capabilities without the need to use military force. The most famous offensive cyber attack is the Stuxnet virus launched on Iran's nuclear facility at Natanz in 2009. The attack software developed by the U.S. and Israel destroyed 1,000 uranium centrifuges (but also signaled the control room that all was well during the attack) and set back the Iranian nuclear effort by about a year. The result: no lives lost and more time for diplomacy to solve one of the world's most challenging nuclear proliferation problems.

Staying Airborne

You're buckled in, ready for take-off and smooth sailing at 30,000 feet with the airline's entertainment system and Wi-Fi to pass the time. What could go wrong? Cybersecurity experts know! A plane's Wi-Fi or entertainment system could be hacked for tampering with satellite communications and interfering with navigation and control. A tech-savvy hijacker could change your route — or worse — without worrying about getting through airport security to board the plane. While airlines already have robust 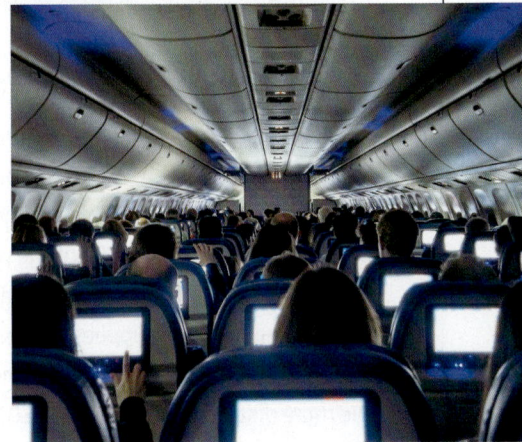 systems in place, and pilots can always take control away from autopilot, without cybersecurity vigilance, passengers could experience more than a bumpy flight.

Shielding Our Schools

The Department of Education recently issued a warning to K-12 educators and parents of the threat posed by hackers. Cyber criminals see schools as only minimally effective at protecting information and easy prey for extortion by malware and ransomware. According to the Wall Street Journal, cyber thieves have targeted more than 36 school systems nationwide, stealing paychecks and social security numbers, or taking over networks and demanding large ransoms. Schools are putting defenses in place, but clearly more is needed.

cybersecurity is

Maintaining Access to Energy

There is still plenty of oil for powering the global economy but a cyber intrusion into the petroleum supply system could change that. That's why the 2012 cyber attacks on the production and safety systems of Saudi Aramco, the state-owned company that produces 10% of the world's oil, drew so much attention. The 2012 attack was massive, wiping out 35,000 computers, disrupting oil transport, and threatening world oil supplies. The hackers, who may have been connected to Iran, were never identified, and Aramco went offline to rebuild its IT network. All the more disturbing, then, that in 2016 the Shamoon virus was able to infect six Saudi government computer systems, including in the energy sector.

> Any device connected to the Internet is vulnerable to cyber attacks.
>
> So, how many devices are connected to the Internet?
>
> TODAY:
> **50 billion**
>
> BY 2020:
> **200 billion**

> **COST OF CYBERCRIME**
> TODAY:
> **$3 trillion**
>
> BY 2020:
> **$6 trillion**

Hailing a Safer Ride

Your Uber pulls up, and in you go. It turns out you might need more than a seat belt to keep yourself safe. In 2016, a hacker gained access to the data of 57 million Uber customers, including phone numbers, email addresses, and names of both customers and drivers. Uber kept the breach secret, though, until November 2017. The company paid the hacker a whopping $100,000 to destroy the data as a "bug bounty," money some companies pay to computer experts who help them identify security breaches. However, covering up the breach and destroying the data could put Uber on the wrong side of laws about how companies must handle personal data and violations of privacy. And it cost two senior employees their jobs. This bug has delivered quite a bite.

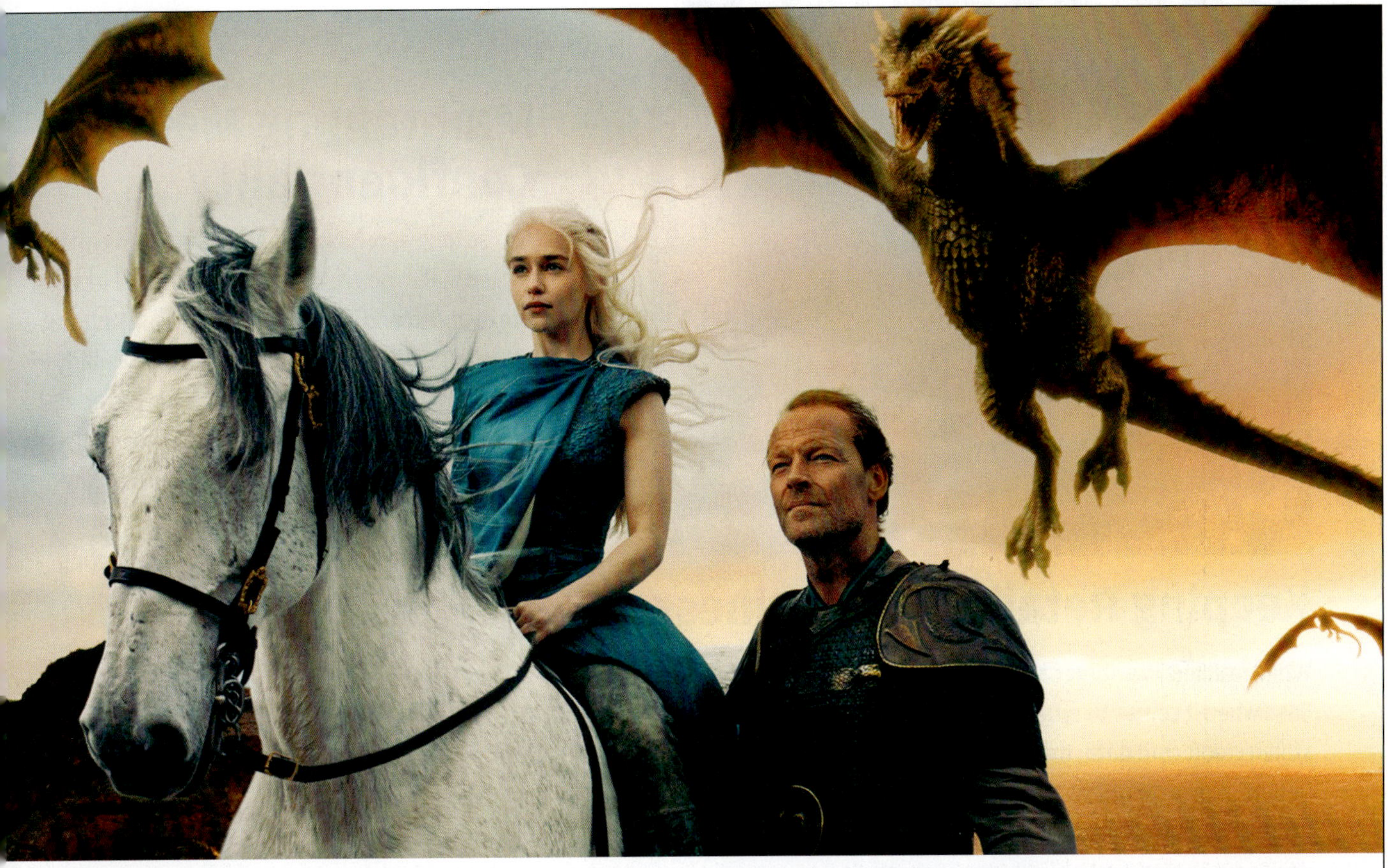

Calling "Cut" on Entertainment Hacks

While money, not safety, is at stake in Hollywood hacks, it's a lot of money — which translates into jobs, as well as profits. A Sony Pictures hack cost the company $100 million dollars, and Disney has not disclosed what it paid in ransom in an attack on its "Pirates of the Caribbean" franchise. HBO's "Game of Thrones" became the hottest celebrity victim of a cyber attack when Iranian hackers stole and aired a new episode online, and hackers aired 10 episodes of "Orange is the New Black" after Netflix refused to pay a ransom. Hollywood is especially vulnerable to code theft and hacking because of the number of people involved in making every movie and TV show. Since production teams need to collaborate, passwords get passed around, and many employees are freelancers using their own computers and software. Winter will be coming to Hollywood a lot sooner if it can't protect itself from the blizzard of cyber attacks.

Helping Hotels Stay Safe

In recent years, the IT systems of some of the world's biggest hotel chains were hacked. Guests' personal information is stored in computers in multiple hotel departments, such as restaurants, amenities, and the front desk, so hotels offer hackers multiple targets. Hotels also usually collect driver's licenses or passport information in combination with credit card data, making identity theft easy once a hacker gets into the system. Given the function of a hotel, hacking into the computer system that holds financial records can give cyber criminals access to the operations of door locks, heating and air-conditioning, and electrical and plumbing systems. Closing the door on hackers requires daily cybersecurity housekeeping!

SHUTTERSTOCK; ISTOCKPHOTO.COM (2); COURTESY HBO

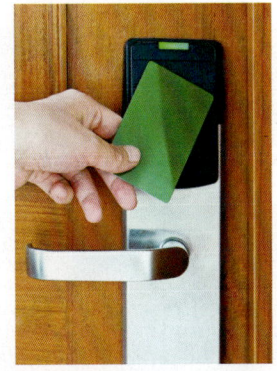

cybersecurity is

Keeping Retailers in Business

While retailers like Target and Home Depot capture the headlines when it comes to cyber attacks due to the volume of the stolen credit card data, the Cisco 2017 Annual Cybersecurity Report makes clear that the entire industry is under continuous attack. Nearly one in three retailers has sustained revenue loss due to cyber attacks. Ironically, because retailers boost revenues by improving operations with technology, in so doing they expose themselves and their customers to theft. Both Main Street shops and Big Box stores face the same challenge of keeping information shoplifters out of their cyber space.

Maintaining Medical Confidentiality

Not so long ago, hospital records were on paper locked in file rooms. Today, most hospital records are digitized and locked in IT systems. Electronic record-keeping creates efficiencies, particularly in the exchange of information between providers and insurers. But it has also exposed hospitals and their patients to a variety of ills. According to reports, during 2016 there was at least one health-related data breach per day — affecting a total of more than 27 million patient records. Hackers can commit insurance fraud with stolen health data as well as identity theft. Also, using ransomware, hackers have held hospitals' data hostage, risking hospital services and potentially patients' lives. Without investment in cybersecurity, the health industry could face a hacking pandemic.

Deterring Industrial Espionage

The typical corporate spy used to be a rogue employee with a briefcase, spiriting out paper records of the trade secrets he had personal access to for sale to a wily competitor. Technology raised the stakes, and corporate espionage has only become more threatening with IT development. Today, the information systems of global corporations contain intellectual property worth billions of dollars and essential to a nation's competitiveness or defense. All of it is at risk not only from disgruntled employees but also from organized crime and foreign competitors and adversaries. According to General Keith Alexander, the former Commander of the U.S. Cyber Command, "the loss of industrial information and intellectual property through cyber espionage constitutes the greatest transfer of wealth in history." It is also a major security risk.

Driving Improvements

Imagine a world in which overtired, distracted, and drunk drivers don't exist; highway deaths would plummet! Google, General Motors, Tesla, and other major car manufacturers are racing to ramp up production of driverless cars, so that by 2020, America can start to reap the benefits of this exciting new technology. But before the driverless car industry can hit the gas, it needs to address the threat of cyber attacks. A computer-driven car connected to satellite GPS technology is a target as much as transport. Just a few years ago, a team of experts hacked the network of a semi-autonomous Jeep Cherokee and killed the transmission, instantly stopping the vehicle. Now imagine ransomware doing that to you — or to a truck with a cargo of HAZMAT. The road to autonomous vehicles will be far from smooth without cybersecurity driving development.

DID YOU KNOW?

1. Cybersecurity isn't just coding and programming. It's also drafting and implementing cyber policies for secure information exchange and storage. And cybersecurity is digital forensics for finding how who did what, where, and when — in order to stop them in the future.

2. The most important skills for success in a cyber job aren't necessarily tech-related. Communication skills are commonly seen as being extremely important.

3. Women and minorities make great cybersecurity experts because they tend to come from diverse personal and academic backgrounds and bring broad perspectives to analysis, teamwork, and problem-solving.

SOURCE: NEW AMERICAN FOUNDATION

educational pathways

There are many options for starting and advancing in careers within cybersecurity. Pick a path that works for you.

Keep in mind that 83% of job postings ask for a bachelor's degree or higher.

HIGH SCHOOL
See page 18 for more info

GET A CYBERSECURITY CERTIFICATION
See page 22 for more info

GET A 2-YEAR ASSOCIATE'S DEGREE
See page 26 for more info

GET 4-YEAR BACHELOR'S DEGREE
See page 30 for more info

ENTRY-LEVEL POSITIONS	AVERAGE SALARY
IT Support Specialist (Computer Network Support Specialist)	$40,000
Associate Cybersecurity Analyst (Junior Analyst)	$37,900

To advance further, you'll need an associate's degree or bachelor's degree.

ENTRY-LEVEL POSITIONS	AVERAGE SALARY
Network Support Specialist (Network Administrator; System Administrator or Security Administrator; Computer Support Technician)	$48,000
Computer Forensics Analyst	$59,000
Cybersecurity Specialist	$60,000

WITH WORK EXPERIENCE	AVERAGE SALARY
Network Support Specialist	$59,000
Computer Forensics Analyst	$89,000
Penetration Tester	$71,929

ENTRY-LEVEL POSITIONS	AVERAGE SALARY
Cybersecurity Specialist/ Technician (Information Security Specialist or IT Specialist)	$81,000
Cybercrime Analyst (Security Analyst - Digital Forensics; Computer Forensics Analyst; Senior Investigative Agent)	$88,000
Incident Analyst/Responder (Senior Analyst, Information Security; Information Security Project Manager; Cyber Defense Center Analyst)	$70,000
IT Auditor (IT Audit Manager)	$85,000

WITH WORK EXPERIENCE	AVERAGE SALARY
Cybersecurity Analyst	$92,000
Penetration Tester	$98,000
Cybersecurity Consultant	$101,000
Cybersecurity Engineer	$107,000
Cybersecurity Manager	$107,000
Cybersecurity Architect	$126,000

SOURCE: CYBERDEGREES.ORG

types of careers

Pick Your Path

Cybersecurity professionals are needed in every industry to protect information systems and data from cyber bad guys. But there are many different types of cybersecurity jobs: "ethical hackers" who test IT systems by trying to break in; threat analysts who look for evidence of system penetration; forensic analysts who investigate how break-ins occurred; recovery specialists who rebuild and recover data; and managers who organize objectives, lead teams, and report on results. The range of job possibilities is literally awesome.

In 2010, The National Institute of Standards and Technology (NIST) launched the National Initiative for Cybersecurity Education (NICE). NICE embraces the Cybersecurity Workforce Framework, which outlines seven functions or capabilities a cybersecurity system must have: **Investigate**, **Collect and Operate**, **Securely Provision**, **Operate and Maintain**, **Analyze**, **Protect and Defend**, and **Oversight and Development**. Take a closer look at what each of these functions includes on the next three pages. Which interests you most? Because some functions overlap, if you start in one job area, you generally can shift to another with some extra training. But there's no need to decide on a job before looking into paths to skills training and options in higher education — all cybersecurity careers start with either certifications or degrees.

ILLUSTRATIONS BY KEVIN MYERS

INVESTIGATE

Investigate, review, and evaluate cyber events and cyber crimes.

WHAT THEY DO
- Investigate cyber crimes
- Recover data from computers to use in prosecuting crimes, analyzing and decrypting any type of hidden information
- Identify and assess cyber criminals or foreign entities
- Help law enforcement and counterintelligence investigations

JOB TITLE EXAMPLES
Forensic Computer Analyst
Cryptographer
Cyber Intelligence Analyst
Security Analyst

DEGREE OR TRAINING
Cybersecurity
Computer Science
Network Security
Information Assurance
Forensic Science
IT and Security

COLLECT AND OPERATE

Collect, process, analyze, and present information from adversaries that may be used to develop intelligence and counterintelligence.

WHAT THEY DO
- Collect intelligence, and interpret and analyze information
- Discover and mitigate criminal and adversarial threats

JOB TITLE EXAMPLES
Cyber Analyst
Intelligence Analyst
Information Systems Manager
Security Software Developer

ADVANCED DEGREE OR TRAINING
Cybersecurity
Computer Science or Engineering
IT or Network Security

SECURELY PROVISION

Conceptualize, design, and build secure IT systems.

WHAT THEY DO
- Create tools for virus, spyware, or malware detection
- Prevent intrusions to computer systems
- Analyze and test computer applications or software
- Technology research and development
- Determine systems requirements and development
- Test and evaluate systems

JOB TITLE EXAMPLES
Computer Programmer
Computer Systems Analyst
Software Developer
Systems Engineer
Information Assurance Developer
Network Security Analyst
Systems Security Architect
Information Technology Director

DEGREE OR TRAINING
Computer Science
Networking
Electrical Engineering
Systems Engineering

types of careers

OPERATE AND MAINTAIN

Provide support, administration, and maintenance necessary to ensure effective and efficient IT system performance and security. Of all the roles, this one has the most job openings.

WHAT THEY DO
- Develop, support, and maintain databases and networks
- Manage intellectual capital and content
- Install, configure, test, operate, maintain and manage network server configurations, access, firewalls, and patches

JOB TITLE EXAMPLES
Customer/Technical Support Specialist
Data or Database Specialist
Information Systems Security Engineer
Network Specialist
System Administrator

DEGREE OR TRAINING
Computer Science
Information Technology
Network/Computer Systems

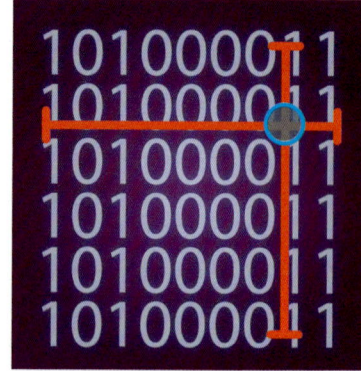

ANALYZE

Responsible for expert review and evaluation of incoming cybersecurity information to determine its usefulness for intelligence.

WHAT THEY DO
- Identify and assess the capabilities and activities of cyber criminals or foreign entities
- Produce findings to help initialize or support law enforcement and counterintelligence investigations or activities
- Analyze threat information from multiple sources, disciplines, and agencies across the intelligence community.

JOB TITLE EXAMPLES
Cyber Threat Analyst
Cyber Counter Intelligence Analyst
Cryptanalysis and Signals Analyst
Security Analyst

ADVANCED DEGREE OR TRAINING
Computer Science
Criminal Justice
Forensics
Information Technology
Engineering
Law

WHO DONE IT?

A **digital forensics expert** examines an IT system just as a medical forensics scientist examines a dead body! As noted forensic computer examiner Eric Robi says, "a computer forensic analyst has to be incredibly curious about how computers work and how people behave." In addition to curiosity and insight, you will be expected to have strong written and oral communication skills. A large part of an expert's job is devoted to writing reports and explaining evidence.

In the case of criminal prosecutions, you need be able to explain your findings before lawyers, judges, and juries who lack tech backgrounds. Can you defend your findings when cross-examined by opposing counsel? Whether you are speaking to intelligence partners, corporate clients, or law enforcement, you need to be able to be crystal clear!

SOURCE: CYBERDEGREES.ORG: BECOME A FORENSICS EXPERT

PROTECT AND DEFEND

Identify, analyze, and prevent cyber threats to an organization.

WHAT THEY DO
- Look for weaknesses in your software, hardware, and networks and find creative ways to protect it
- Respond to incidents
- Manage and monitor networks to remediate unauthorized activities
- Conduct assessments of threats and vulnerabilities

JOB TITLE EXAMPLES
Ethical Hacker
Incident Responder
Penetration Tester
Intelligence Analyst
Security Analyst
Chief Information Security Officer

DEGREE OR TRAINING
Computer Science
Cybersecurity
Information Assurance
IT and Security
Network Security

CALLING ALL (ETHICAL) HACKERS

A penetration tester (a.k.a., ethical hacker) probes for and then exploits security vulnerabilities in web-based applications, networks, and systems. In other words, you're paid to hack — and it's legal! Using a series of penetration tools, some that you will design yourself, you simulate real-life cyber attacks, perhaps taking part in Red Team/Blue Team exercises that mimic cyber warfare. Your ultimate aim is to help an organization improve its cybersecurity. Most pen testers don't hold a specialized degree. Since ethical hacking is more about skills than course credits, a bachelor's or master's degree in cybersecurity may be unnecessary if you have the right experience.

SOURCE: LOUDPROGRAMER.NET: 9 SKILLS THAT WILL GET YOU A JUNIOR PENETRATION TESTER JOB

OVERSIGHT AND DEVELOPMENT

Provide leadership, management, direction, and/or development and advocacy so that individuals and organizations may effectively conduct cyber security work.

WHAT THEY DO
- Offer legal or policy assistance
- Manage the technical direction and strategic plan for an organization
- May include e-commerce, privacy, copyright, and intellectual property

JOB TITLE EXAMPLES
Chief Information Officer
Cyber Security Trainer
Lawyer or Legal Advisor
Policy Analyst

ADVANCED DEGREE OR TRAINING
Business
Criminal Justice
Information Technology
Law

education: High School

Get Ready: 7 Things To Do Now

Making smart decisions in high school will pay off later.

Given the increasing number, diversity, and complexity of information systems, cybersecurity is one of the most exciting career areas out there. Any cybersecurity career requires a credential or degree of some kind, but there are two-year, four-year, and graduate school possibilities, as well as certifications and higher education online. Rather than sweat those details now, take these steps in high school to keep your options open.

1. Take plenty of math classes. As far as preparation goes, the first and last word is math, so cover algebra through calculus, to the highest level possible. Does your school offer computer science or statistics? If you can, take those courses, but prioritize the fundamentals, including physics.

2. Don't shelve English. Keep writing and critical thinking classes like social studies in your school schedule because you'll need to be able to communicate all your great ideas.

3. Learn basic coding. If your school doesn't offer coding classes, there are FREE online computer science and coding classes (see page 23 for more information). Check out Code Academy, Alison.com, and Kahn Academy. Or enroll in online courses with a not-for-profit college.

4. Build your own website. Once you have a basic knowledge of coding, build your own site by yourself or with friends to gain experience programming. You could even try building a home computer network.

5. Go out for the team. As Dr. Margaret Leary of Northern Virginia Community College observes, most cybersecurity careers require working independently but as part of a team, using skills best

learned by doing. Colleges — and employers — look for participation on robotics teams and in computer and cybersecurity competitions, like CyberPatriot (see page 20). If your school lacks these, resources such as NOVALabs and Hour of Code offer online communities for games and competitions. Start a cyber club at your school if there isn't one. Engineering organizations like the Institute of Electrical and Electronics Engineers (IEEE) Computer Society can help direct you to a local mentor. Local colleges and universities often host activities for high school students interested in computer science and cyber careers, so contact them directly and ask your school counselor to help you.

6. Use summer for cyber. A basic job that has you working with computers and abiding by security rules boosts your college resume. IEEE or a simple online search will help you find internships and computing skills camps near you. The National Security Agency (NSA) runs the GenCyber Camp program, which is based at colleges nationwide. And if none of these options works for you, those FREE online activities you didn't have time for during the school year will fit into any summer schedule! The NSA's game Day of Cyber mimics a day in the life of a cybersecurity professional in just 2-3 hours.

7. Be good. Whatever else you do, whether in school or out, avoid unethical computing and social media activities. Or anything unethical, for that matter. Cybersecurity professionals operate in the most sensitive areas of government and private industry, for which security clearances are required. You need to demonstrate integrity and good judgment, not just good skills.

education: Competitions and Contests

Let the Games Begin!

Competitions like CyberPatriot don't require prior knowledge of cybersecurity but can teach you volumes while you're having fun.

Competitions are more than just a good time. Community colleges, universities, and employers take a serious interest in them because competitions develop real skills in cyber problem-solving. You don't need prior knowledge, and participating in competitions shows you have real interest in cybersecurity and in your own skills development. Also, major public and private sector employers collaborate in sponsoring competitions and financially support student participation. They also award scholarships and are sources for internships.

CyberPatriot is a national competition created by the Air Force Association (AFA) in 2009 and sponsored by Northrop Grumman and the NSA. CyberPatriot is now famous for being the most fun competition in cyberspace. The program is structured for all levels of experience in middle and high school — including none! The tournament is held via the Internet, over several months during weekends. Local and state rounds of elimination culminate in the national round, an in-person challenge event held in Baltimore, MD.

Teams are limited to six kids and fall into three divisions: Open High School Division, which includes home schools and groups such as the Boys and Girls Club, the Boy and Girl Scouts, and other youth groups; All Service Division, open to JROTC and other cadet corps units; and Middle School Division, also open to all schools and youth groups. Teams download an information system with bugs and security vulnerabilities and are timed in the process of finding them. Points are awarded for maintaining functionality and correctly identifying problems — points are deducted for incorrect assessments and function drops. The final rounds include challenges in network security design and digital forensics.

Mary Pearse, Communications Coordinator with AFA, notes that in 2016, 5,500 teams participated, together with coaches, mentors, and judges — all of whom, says Pearse, love the intensity of the competition and willingly stay up all night to complete scoring. AFA encourages and tracks involvement by girls and minorities, and Pearse is proud to say that CyberPatriot has above average participation by all-girl teams.

There are other competitions out there! Mitre hosts the Capture the Flag Cyber Challenge with college level as well as high school teams. The Department of Homeland Security (DHS) sponsors the U.S. Cyber Challenge together with the non-profit Center for Information Security. So, if you're curious about cybersecurity, a competition might be a good place to start!

education: Cybersecurity Certification

Coastline Community College, CA

California State University-San Bernardino

Montgomery College, MD

Jump-Start Your Career

Obtain a cybersecurity certification and start working, but continue your education to maximize career options.

Certifications in computing are skills-focused credentials for entry-level cybersecurity employment or preparation for higher education. They are widely and inexpensively available, including online. If your high school offers computer science, you may nevertheless lack tech skills you'll need to work on an information system. Certificate programs make up for this, and if you plan to work while going to school, you'll need certification to be employable.

But what kind? While no previous work experience is required, you'll need to build from the basics up. Certifications are sometimes called Network Security or Information Assurance. No matter what the name, however, make sure you are using an accredited program for a recognized certificate.

University of Colorado, Colorado Springs

FREE ONLINE CYBER CLASSES

Yes! You can take FREE cyber classes through MOOCs (Massive Open Online Courses), which are offered by universities and available to anyone interested in cybersecurity.

In many universities, MOOCs are basically "teasers," albeit teasers with great instructors and solid content. The idea is to get you excited about the subject and interested in the university's fee-based programs. Because they're free and self-directed, you won't receive college credit for MOOCs. You may be able to get a certificate of completion, but that usually comes with a price tag. Classes are offered throughout the calendar year, but check the university's schedule because even online classes usually have fixed starting dates.

FORMAT: Video lectures are usually pre-recorded, although instructors interact with students in virtual forums, live chats, and/or during virtual office hours.

TIME COMMITMENT: Like many online courses, cybersecurity MOOCs take 6-10 weeks. Overall, you can expect to devote 3-6 hours of your life per week to each course.

ASSESSMENT: There are no fixed rules on assessment. There may be peer-to-peer reviews among students and interactive class discussions or hands-on projects capped by a final exam. Many cybersecurity MOOCs incorporate programming labs and regular quizzes to test comprehension. Make no mistake, it's a real course, with real effort required!

SOURCE: CYBERDEGREES.ORG

CompTIA offers the Security+ certificate for entry-level employment in network installation and maintenance. Getting the Security+ doesn't demand many hours, and it's the foundation for other certifications. ISACA, a non-profit involved in cybersecurity, offers many security-related cyber certificates, including the more advanced CISM, Certified Information Security Manager. Another more advanced — and very hot — credential is EC Council's CEH Ethical Hacker Certificate.

Apart from giving you a credential you can put to use as soon as you have it, certifications can be earned by self-study or in classes. The University of Maryland Baltimore Campus offers classes for the CompTIA Security+ and financial aid is available. The National Cybersecurity Institute also has classes, some of which are free, that can prepare you for certificate studies.

To figure out what you are eligible to take, use websites to read up on what the certificates equip you to do and find out the prerequisites. There are also cybersecurity bootcamps offered by a number of certifiers. The National Cybersecurity Institute, the American National Standards Institute, ISACA, the Committee on National Security Systems, and IEEE Computer Society are all good sources of information on cyber certificates that meet standards for employment and a simple "near me" Google search will raise options on where to study.

education: Cybersecurity Certification

Mohawk Valley Community College, NY

City College of San Francisco

WHERE TO GET CYBER CERT

For students who want to prepare for an entry-level job in cybersecurity without completing all the coursework required for an associate's degree or a bachelor's degree, a certification is a good first step. No previous work experience is required. The certifications are sometimes called Network Security or Information Assurance. Some courses are offered only online, others are a combination of on campus and online. Schools that offer classes online are marked with an asterisk.

ALABAMA
Snead State Community College

ARIZONA
Mohave Community College

ARKANSAS
University of Arkansas at Little Rock

CALIFORNIA
California State University-Fullerton
California State University-San Bernardino*
City College of San Francisco
Coastline Community College
Los Medanos College
Monterey Peninsula College
Sacramento City College

COLORADO
Front Range Community College
University of Colorado, Colorado Springs

CONNECTICUT
Capital Community College

FLORIDA
Palm Beach State College
Pasco-Hernando State College
University of West Florida*
Valencia College

GEORGIA
Armstrong State University
Augusta University
Georgia Regents University
Kennesaw State University

HAWAII
Honolulu Community College

IDAHO
College of Western Idaho

ILLINOIS
Elmhurst College*
Joliet Junior College
Illinois Institute of Technology*
McHenry County College
Moraine Valley Community College
Rock Valley College
Shawnee Community College

INDIANA
Indiana University-Purdue University-Indianapolis
Ivy Tech Community College*

IOWA
Des Moines Area Community College
Northeast Iowa Community College-Calmar

KANSAS
Butler Community College

KENTUCKY
Kentucky Community and Technical College System*
Kentucky State University

LOUISIANA
Bossier Parish Community College

MARYLAND
Anne Arundel Community College*
Community College of Baltimore County*
Capitol Technology University
Hagerstown Community College
Harford Community College
Howard Community College
Montgomery College
Prince George's Community College

MASSACHUSETTS
Massachusetts Bay Community College
Mount Wachusett Community College

Moraine Valley Community College, IL

FICATES

MICHIGAN
Central Michigan University*
Oakland Community College
Wayne County Community College District

MINNESOTA
Lake Superior College*
Normandale Community College
Quinsigamond Community College*

MISSOURI
Fontbonne University*

NEBRASKA
Bellevue University*
Northeast Community College

NEVADA
College of Southern Nevada

NEW HAMPSHIRE
NHTI-Concord's Community College
River Valley Community College
White Mountains Community College

NEW JERSEY
New Jersey City University

NEW MEXICO
Central New Mexico Community College
Eastern New Mexico University-Ruidoso

NEW YORK
Erie Community College
Mohawk Valley Community College
SUNY Westchester Community College

NORTH CAROLINA
Beaufort County Community College
Central Carolina Community College
Craven Community College*
Edgecombe Community College
Fayetteville Technical Community College
Forsyth Technical Community College*
Gaston College
Rowan-Cabarrus Community College

OHIO
Kent State University at Kent
Owens Community College
Sinclair Community College

OKLAHOMA
Oklahoma City Community College
Rose State College

OREGON
Chemeketa Community College
Linfield College*
Mt Hood Community College

PENNSYLVANIA
Montgomery County Community College

SOUTH CAROLINA
Horry-Georgetown Technical College
Piedmont Technical College
Trident Technical College

TENNESSEE
Nashville State Community College

TEXAS
Amarillo College
Central Texas College*
Houston Community College
Richland College
San Antonio College
South Texas College
St Philip's College
TEEX Cybersecurity at Texas A&M*
Temple College
Texas State Technical College-System

UTAH
Salt Lake Community College

VIRGINIA
Lord Fairfax Community College
Northern Virginia Community College*
Thomas Nelcon Community College
Tidewater Community College

WASHINGTON
Edmonds Community College
Highline Community College
Whatcom Community College
Washington Adventist University

WEST VIRGINIA
American Military University*
Blue Ridge Community and Technical College

WISCONSIN
Fox Valley Technical College
Madison Area Technical College
Milwaukee Area Technical College
Moraine Park Technical College*
University of Wisconsin-Parkside
Waukesha County Technical College

WYOMING
Casper College
Sheridan College

education: Community Colleges

Two-Year Plan

Community colleges offer cybersecurity associate's degrees and certifications, enabling students to get into the workforce quickly.

San Anton College, T

County College of Morris, NY

Oakland Community College, MI

Community college cybersecurity certificate programs prepare students for working and also support continuing on to bachelor's degrees. There are campus-based programs and online classes. Students may be still in high school, just out of high school, or at any stage of a career that may or may not already include cybersecurity. The diversity of options and students means community college education offers more than just low tuition costs. Community colleges prioritize hands-on skills for employment with minimal need for on-the-job training. Employers love this!

The AAS, Associate of Applied Science, offers a variety of concentrations, all of which give students practical skills needed to work in an existing information system. Areas include threat analysis, monitoring a system for indicators of compromise or penetration in light of new hacking technology, and digital forensics analysis to determine who hacked a system and how in order to prevent future compromise. To a lesser extent, students also study the engineering of computer hardware and software. AAS certificate holders are immediately employable, and the education in technology development equips them to pursue bachelor's degrees.

Dr. Margaret Leary, director of curriculum at the National CyberWatch Center and a professor at Northern Virginia Community College (NOVA), says that

Northern Virginia Community College

Santa Fe Community College, FL

colleges offer scholarships to students with the AAS certificate. Marymount University in Northern Virginia offers both bachelor's and master's of science degrees in cybersecurity, potentially on full scholarship for AAS graduates.

Community colleges include students of all backgrounds and ages, many of whom work. Most cybersecurity work is performed by teams in which every member is responsible for tasks and accountable to other team members. Community college students learn how to communicate and collaborate with people different from themselves and tend quickly to develop the professionalism that employers expect by interacting with their classmates.

Great opportunities for apprenticeships are another advantage to community college education — and apprenticeships with government agencies include a basic security clearance. All cybersecurity careers demand the highest standards of personal integrity and most require security credentials. Even in private industry, having a government security clearance shows you can be trusted, so an apprenticeship with a government agency enhances employability everywhere. Normally, the process of obtaining a government security clearance from a standard job application takes months, which means months waiting and not working. Community college programs can be the fast track to an important career credential.

Finally, working in cybersecurity demands that you show you can be trusted. Behaviors that indicate poor judgment or create vulnerability to pressure from bad actors, like hackers, foreign governments, or criminal enterprises, are red flags. Problems like big credit card bills, careless use of social media, or recreational drug use can get in the way of a future in cybersecurity.

Bachelor of Science degree programs are paying attention to the AAS programs developed at community colleges. Demand for professionals who can perform analysis in cybersecurity is high, especially in the federal government. Most community college graduates continue their education at some point, however, because bachelor's degrees are important for long-term career development. George Mason University, a partner with NOVA, has created a Bachelor of Applied Science degree specifically to align with the AAS. Even better, many four-year

education: Community Colleges

Herkimer County Community College, NY

Montgomery College, MD

COLLEGES OFFERING CYBER A

This list may not be definitive as degree programs are being added regularly.

ALABAMA
Northeast Alabama Community College
Snead State Community College

ARIZONA
Estrella Mountain Community College
Mohave Community College

CALIFORNIA
Coastline Community College
California Institute of Arts & Technology*
City College of San Francisco
Los Medanos College
Sacramento City College

COLORADO
Arapahoe Community College
Front Range Community College
Pikes Peak Community College
Red Rocks Community College

FLORIDA
Florida State College at Jacksonville
Santa Fe College
St. Petersburg College*
Valencia College

HAWAII
Honolulu Community College

IDAHO
North Idaho College

ILLINOIS
College of DuPage
Joliet Junior College
Moraine Valley Community College
Rock Valley College
Shawnee Community College

INDIANA
Ivy Tech Community College

IOWA
Des Moines Area Community College

KANSAS
Butler Community College
Manhattan Area Technical College

KENTUCKY
Sullivan University*

LOUISIANA
Bossier Parish Community College

MAINE
University of Maine at Fort Kent*

MARYLAND
Anne Arundel Community College
Baltimore City Community College
College of Southern Maryland
Community College of Baltimore County
Hagerstown Community College
Harford Community College
Howard Community College
Montgomery College
Prince George's Community College

MASSACHUSETTS
Massachusetts Bay Community College*
Quinsigamond Community College*

MICHIGAN
Henry Ford College
Bay de Noc Community College
Macomb Community College
Mott Community College
Oakland Community College
Wayne County Community
   College District

MINNESOTA
Lake Superior College*

Westchester Community College, NY

OCIATES' DEGREES

Minneapolis Community and Technical College
Minnesota State College-Southeast Technical*
Minnesota West Community and Technical College*

MISSOURI
St. Charles Community College
St. Louis Community College

NEBRASKA
Northeast Community College
Southeast Community College Area*
Western Nebraska Community College*

NEVADA
College of Southern Nevada

NEW HAMPSHIRE
River Valley Community College

NEW JERSEY
County College of Morris

NEW MEXICO
Eastern New Mexico University-Ruidoso

NEW YORK
Erie Community College
Mohawk Valley Community College
Rockland Community College
Herkimer County Community College
Westchester Community College
SUNY Westchester Community College

NORTH CAROLINA
Asheville-Buncombe Technical Community College
Fayetteville Technical Community College
Forsyth Technical Community College
Gaston College
Rowan-Cabarrus Community College

NORTH DAKOTA
Bismarck State College*

OHIO
Clark State Community College
Sinclair Community College
Terra State Community College

OKLAHOMA
Francis Tuttle Technology School
Oklahoma City Community College
Oklahoma Department of Career & Technology Career Centers
Rose State College
Oklahoma State University Institute of Technology-Okmulgee*

PENNSYLVANIA
Pennsylvania College of Technology

OREGON
Mt. Hood Community College
Linn Benton Community College
Umpqua Community College*

SOUTH DAKOTA
Dakota State University*

TENNESSEE
Jackson State Community College
Fountainhead College of Technology
National College*

TEXAS
Amarillo College
Central Texas College*
Cuyamaca College*
El Paso Community College
Houston Community College
Richland College
San Antonio College
South Texas College
St. Philip's College*

VIRGINIA
Danville Community College
ECPI University*
Lord Fairfax Community College
Northern Virginia Community College
Tidewater Community College

WASHINGTON
Clover Park Technical College
Columbia Basin College
Highline College
Whatcom Community College

WEST VIRGINIA
Blue Ridge Community and Technical College

WISCONSIN
Fox Valley Technical College
Madison Area Technical College
Milwaukee Area Technical College
Waukesha County Technical College

WYOMING
Casper College
Sheridan College

*Online

education: Colleges and Universities

Four Years of Cyber

A cyber degree at any of the nation's universities is a great investment in your future.

You've decided you want to head straight for a bachelor's degree, so what is there to know about college and university programs in cybersecurity?

A cybersecurity degree is a Bachelor of Science in a program that combines computer science or similar engineering coursework with classes that develop computing skills. This degree prepares students to analyze the structure of a computer system on an ongoing basis, looking into whether it has been compromised, and eliminating vulnerabili-

University of Maryland, College Park

ties. Being able to do this depends as much on having computing skills as on knowing the underlying computer science. So in looking for a cyber degree program, look for programs with coursework and labs in both science and skills, together with extracurricular opportunities for competitions and also internships that develop practical experience.

The National Security Agency (NSA) has accredited college and university programs as National Centers of Academic Excellence in Cyber Operations, CAE-CO. These schools offer cybersecurity degree programs that include coursework in science and engineering, the technology of cyber operations, and additional cyber-learning activities. Because the federal government is the largest employer of cybersecurity professionals, it makes sense that many schools in Maryland and Virginia are CAE-CO accredited. But CAE-CO programs are found in public and private colleges and universities literally all over the U.S. And programs not CAE-CO designated are equally recognized by employers and graduate schools, provided they cover the combination of course work and extracurricular activities offered by CAE-CO programs.

It's obvious that cybersecurity is critical in intelligence and defense. Yet because cybersecurity is also important to healthcare and finance industries, commerce and other business activities (see pages 4-11), degree programs all over the country have developed focuses for coursework and research — and partnerships with employers. The University of Southern California has ties to Silicon Valley as well as to the defense industry. Georgia's Kennesaw State University offers programs directed at cyber forensics, finance, and healthcare. Syracuse University in New York offers concentrations in cyber technology and finance, among others. Ohio State University is engaged in research on smart grids and mobile phone technology, while the University of Cincinnati has won grants from the World Bank for cyber operations research.

Champlain University undergraduate Brendan Gordy is majoring in digital forensics. His degree program includes cybersecurity and criminal justice coursework, with the goal of joining the Internet Crimes Against Children Task Force. Digital forensics is a vital element in law enforcement, answering the what, who, and how questions in computer-based crime, to figure out what happened, apprehend those responsible, and prevent future abuses. Brendan describes himself as good at computers but not really interested in programming. Champlain, in Vermont and among the top universities in cybersecurity education, offers labs to develop hands-on skills in criminal investigation based on actual past cases. And the Leahy Center for Digital Investigations is

education: Colleges and Universities

US Naval Academy's new center for cybersecurity studies, set to open in 2019

The Nation's Military Academies Lead the Way

Winning the war of the future will take more than better codes and faster digital hardware. The U.S. needs leaders to fend off mounting cyber attacks and to launch cyber attacks on our enemies.

The U.S. Military Academy, Air Force Academy, Naval Academy, and Coast Guard Academy all offer accredited CAE-CO cybersecurity degree programs. Cadets and Midshipmen take courses in technology, such as computer architecture, networks, database systems, and cryptography but also develop leadership skills. Programs also require coursework in policy, law, and ethics, to ensure that each student gains understanding of the nuances of cyber warfare. Each academy's cybersecurity program prepares future officers for cyber-related assignments, including in all the military cyber commands, and for advanced studies.

While learning the tools of cyber craft in the classroom is an important first step, students need as much real-world experience as possible. That's why in 2001 the National Security Agency launched the Cyber Defense Exercise competition specifically for teams from the military academies plus teams from the U.S. Coast Guard Academy, U.S. Merchant Marine Academy, and the Royal Military College of Canada. Modeled on Red Team/Blue Team simulations, NSA cyber professionals attack the networks of each of the teams. The team that most effectively defends their computer network wins the competition. Last year the Naval Academy won the competition, but all of the competitors were able to learn what they did wrong and how to defend the nation's computer networks.

SOURCE: US NAVAL ACADEMY

available for work/study and internships that entail working on actual open criminal investigations.

The schools mentioned here are just a few of many. We provide a list of schools offering cybersecurity degrees by state on the next two pages and NSA.gov links to the list of CAE-CO programs. Look for internships on the websites of schools that interest you.

And be aware that not all careers in cybersecurity demand the cybersecurity degree! Cybersecurity careers embrace more than using hard skills to work on information systems. Increasingly, employers in both government and private industry need employees with strong skills in communication and critical-thinking. The question employers ask graduates is not "can you code?" but "do you have the hard and soft skills for the job?" — which may be managing a cybersecurity team or a project and include drafting strategic plans or policy analyses.

Math, engineering, psychology, public policy, law enforcement, and other majors can all be the basis for a cybersecurity career so long as you also cover tech fundamentals in your degree program and extracurricular activities. Or major in cybersecurity but make sure to include unrelated coursework in communication, policy, and management. Increasingly, public-sector cybersecurity entails working in multi-agency task forces which may include local, state, and national entities. And cybersecurity work in both government and private industry is international. Your skill set needs to equip you for thinking and collaborating outside the box!

University of Washington, Seattle

Internships: A Rewarding Experience

Apprenticeships and internships are important ways to explore career possibilities and build up skills. We use the term internship here, but apprenticeships and work-study offer the same advantages — and many come with a paycheck!

Because most bachelor's degree programs tend to weight theory over practice, bachelor's degree students really benefit from learning and practicing workplace skills. An internship can boost coding and programming that are light in a degree program, such as math, or make up for computing activities unavailable in your high school.

With their emphasis on teaching hands-on computing skills, community college programs often build relationships with government agencies and businesses to support students gaining work experience while in school. Look for these when you consider which community college to attend. Whether you are in a two-year or four-year degree program, however, most internships require completing a first year of studies or a computing certification. Some demand a specific grade point average. Internships are competitive, so investigate requirements at the outset of your studies.

Among private-sector companies offering cybersecurity internships to undergraduates are Northrop Grumman, Boeing, Booz Allen, IBM, MITRE, Symantec, and Palo Alto Networks — and also Google, Amazon, Sony, and Starbucks! But many companies offer internships, and they are located all over the country. Government agency internships include the CIA, DHS, NSA, the Department of Energy, National Institutes of Health, and others, both within and outside the intelligence community. Some agencies and companies combine scholarships with internships. The NSA's Stokes Scholarship (see page 37), for example, offers funding for a bachelor's degree combined with an NSA internship every summer that rotates through different agency divisions!

While most internships are less comprehensive, a successful experience with any agency or employer may mean the opportunity to return and gain experience in another career area. Start broadly by using sites like Indeed.com and InfoSecConnect.com, or search using the websites of companies and agencies that interest you. Don't overlook faculty members and school career development resources! If you're not sure what to apply for, develop a basic understanding of what working in various areas of cybersecurity entails. The NIST website links to the NICE Framework of cybersecurity career areas with the capability indicators. You can match these against your interests and strengths. Check out USAjobs.gov and look at job postings. Many of the same skill sets are needed in both public- and private-sector employment, so choose your internship based on skills development and building relationships with potential employers.

Top: Students participating in the Cyber Infrastructure Training and Mentoring internship program at New Mexico State University. Above: MITRE Corporation interns worked on real-world problems.

Internships with government agencies often include a security clearance. (Although lawful permanent residents can be cleared to work in cybersecurity, U.S. citizenship is generally required for a security clearance.) Because clearances easily take over a year to get from a standard job application, government internships are accelerators for a wide range of post-grad employment opportunities. Not only does a government security clearance show every employer that you can be trusted, it is required by companies contracting with the government.

Regardless of government clearances, working in cybersecurity demands personal integrity and good judgment. Any indication of poor judgment or vulnerability to blackmail or temptation from hackers, foreign governments, or criminal enterprises will get in the way of a future in cybersecurity. That means big credit card bills, alcohol abuse, or careless use of social media. And avoid recreational drug use even if you live in a state where it has been legalized. The federal government still requires no use of marijuana within a three-year period for clearance eligibility.

education: Colleges and Universities

SCHOOLS WITH CYBER DEGREES

The schools below offer four-year undergraduate cybersecurity degrees, or computer science degrees with a cybersecurity focus. Another option would to check out engineering schools that offer computer engineering degrees. Other schools offer a minor or certificates in cybersecurity. You could also take classes online. Go to this website to find out more: cyberdegrees.org/listings/bachelors-degrees-online/

ALABAMA
Jacksonville State University
Tuskegee University
University of Alabama in Huntsville
University of South Alabama

ARIZONA
Arizona State University
Embry-Riddle Aeronautical University
University of Advancing Technology

ARKANSAS
Southern Arkansas University

CALIFORNIA
California State Polytechnic University, Pomona
California State University, Sacramento
California State University, San Bernardino
Mt. Sierra University
National University
San Jose State University
University of California, Irvine

COLORADO
Colorado School of Mines
Colorado State University-Pueblo
Colorado Technical University
United States Air Force Academy
University of Colorado, Colorado Springs

CONNECTICUT
Charter Oak State College
University of Connecticut
University of New Haven
Western Connecticut State University

DELAWARE
Wilmington University

DISTRICT OF COLUMBIA
George Washington University

FLORIDA
Daytona State College
Embry-Riddle Aeronautical University, Daytona Beach Campus
Florida Atlantic University
Florida Polytechnic University
Florida State University
Hodges University
Indian River State College
Keiser University
Palm Beach State College
Saint Leo University*
University of Central Florida
University of Florida
University of South Florida
University of West Florida

GEORGIA
Armstrong State University
Augusta University
Columbus State University
Georgia Regents University
Kennesaw State University
Middle Georgia State University
University of North Georgia

HAWAII
University of Hawaii, West Oahu
University of Hawaii, Manoa

IDAHO
College of Western Idaho
Idaho State University

ILLINOIS
DePaul University
Illinois Institute of Technology
Illinois State University
Lewis University
Northeastern Illinois University
Southern Illinois University, Carbondale
University of Illinois, Springfield
University of Illinois, Urbana-Champaign

INDIANA
Indiana University
Purdue University
Purdue University-Northwest

IOWA
University of Dubuque

KANSAS
Fort Hays State University
Kansas State University
Pittsburgh State University
Wichita State University

KENTUCKY
Eastern Kentucky University
Kentucky State University
Sullivan University
University of Louisville

LOUISIANA
Louisiana Tech University
Southern University and A & M College
University of New Orleans

MAINE
Thomas College
University of Maine, Augusta
University of Maine, Fort Kent
University of Southern Maine

MARYLAND
Bowie State University
Capitol Technology University
Frostburg State University
Morgan State University
Towson University
United States Naval Academy
University of Maryland, College Park
University of Maryland-Baltimore County
University of Maryland University College

MASSACHUSETTS
Bay Path University

Boston University
Northeastern University
University of Massachusetts, Amherst
Worcester Polytechnic Institute

MICHIGAN
Baker College
Davenport University
Eastern Michigan University
Ferris State University
Michigan Technological University
Northern Michigan University
University of Detroit Mercy
University of Michigan
University of Michigan-Dearborn
Walsh College

MINNESOTA
Lake Superior College
Metropolitan State University
St. Cloud State University
University of St. Thomas
Walden University

MISSISSIPPI
Mississippi State

MISSOURI
Fontbonne University
Lindenwood University
Saint Louis University-Main Campus
Southeast Missouri State University
University of Central Missouri
University of Missouri- St. Louis
Washington University in St Louis

NEBRASKA
Bellevue University
University of Nebraska, Omaha

NEVADA
University of Nevada, Las Vegas

NEW HAMPSHIRE
Southern New Hampshire University

NEW JERSEY
Fairleigh Dickinson University
Felician College
New Jersey City University
New Jersey Institute of Technology
Rutgers, the State University of New Jersey
Stevens Institute of Technology

NEW MEXICO
National American University
New Mexico Institute of Mining & Technology
New Mexico Tech

NEW YORK
Berkeley College
Excelsior College
Hilbert College
Iona College
Mercy College
New York Institute of Technology
New York University
Pace University
Rochester Institute of Technology
St. John's University
Syracuse University
SUNY at Albany
SUNY Institute of Technology
University at Albany
US Military Academy, West Point
Utica College

NORTH CAROLINA
East Carolina University
University of North Carolina, Charlotte

NORTH DAKOTA
Rasmussen College

OHIO
Franklin University
Ohio State University
University of Cincinnati

OKLAHOMA
Cameron University
Northeastern State University
Oklahoma State University
Oklahoma State University Institute
 of Technology-Okmulgee

OREGON
George Fox University
University of Oregon

PENNSYLVANIA
Bloomsburg University of Pennsylvania
Drexel University
East Stroudsburg University
Indiana University of Pennsylvania
Marywood University
Pennsylvania College of Technology
Pennsylvania State University
Robert Morris University
Saint Vincent College
University of Pittsburgh
West Chester University of Pennsylvania

RHODE ISLAND
Johnson & Wales University
New England Institute of Technology

SOUTH CAROLINA
Limestone College
University of South Carolina-Upstate

SOUTH DAKOTA
Dakota State University

TENNESSEE
Fountainhead College of Technology
Lipscomb University
Tennessee Technological University
University of Tennessee at Chattanooga
University of Memphis

TEXAS
Our Lady of the Lake University
Southern Methodist University
Texas A&M University
Texas A&M University-Corpus Christi
Texas A&M University-San Antonio
University of Texas at Austin
University of Texas at Arlington
University of Texas at San Antonio

UTAH
Brigham Young University
Utah Valley University
Western Governors University

VERMONT
Champlain College
Norwich University

VIRGINIA
ECPI University
George Mason University
Hampton University
James Madison University
Marymount University
Norfolk State University
Virginia Tech

WASHINGTON
City University of Seattle
University of Washington, Seattle
University of Washington-Bothell Campus
Western Washington University

WEST VIRGINIA
Marshall University
Salem International University
University of Charleston
West Virginia University

WISCONSIN
University of Wisconsin-Stout

education: Financial Aid

Cut Your Tuition Bill

With the cost of college continuing to rise, it's more important than ever to find ways to reduce costs.

If you're looking for financial aid, start with scholarships at the schools you are interested in attending. These are usually the most generous. But there are also numerous cybersecurity scholarships from many sources, such as non-profits, foundations, institutions, government organizations, and corporations. Did you know that many available scholarships go unused? So apply for as many as you can!

Websites for almost all government agencies include details on scholarships generally as well as partnerships with non-profits and professional organizations, such as Women Who Code. These organizations often have partnerships with universities and private employers for scholarships, paid internships or both. The National Society of Black Engineers, the Society of Hispanic Professional Engineers and the Society of Women Engineers all offer scholarships.

Ask your high school guidance counselor to help you, but here's a good list to get you started. Note that some scholarships require government service in return for the award.

Center For Cyber Safety and Education Women's Scholarship
Award amount: $40,000
https://www.iamcybersafe.org/

CIA Undergraduate Scholarship Program
Award amount: $18,000 + salary
https://www.cia.gov/careers/student-opportunities/undergraduate-scholarship-program.html

The Colonel Sully H. De Fontaine Scholarship Award
Award amount: $1,200
http://www.afio.com/13_scholarships.htm

David L. Boren Undergraduate Scholarships
Award amount: $20,000
https://www.borenawards.org/scholarships/program-basics/boren-scholarship-basics

ESET Women In Cyber Security Scholarship
Award amount: $5,000
https://www.eset.com/us/about/newsroom/corporate-blog/eset-women-in-cybersecurity-scholarship-now-accepting-applications/

The Women Techmakers Scholars Program
Award amount: $5,000 - $10,000
https://www.womentechmakers.com/scholars

Harold F. Tipton Scholarship
Award amount: $5,000
https://iamcybersafe.org/scholarships/harold-f-tipton-memorial-scholarship/

ICMCP Black Hat Scholarship
Award amount: $50,000 divided among applicants
https://icmcp.org/programs/black-hat-scholarship/

(ISC)² Graduate And Undergraduate Scholarships
Award amount: $5,000
https://iamcybersafe.org/scholarships/undergraduate-scholarships/

Lint Center
Award amount: $500-$1,500
https://www.lintcenter.org/scholarships/

National Science Foundation Scholarship for Service (SFS)
Award amount: $22,500-$34,000
https://www.nsf.gov/funding/pgm_summ.jsp?pims_id=504991

Naval Research Enterprise Internship Program
Award amount: $5,400-$10,800
https://nreip.asee.org/

Navy Information Assurance Scholarship
Award amount: tuition + stipend
http://www.doncio.navy.mil/contentview.aspx?id=535

The Peter Jasin Afio Endowment
Award amount: $4,000
http://www.afio.com/13_scholarships.htm

Raytheon's Women In Cyber Security Scholarship
Award amount: $8,000
https://iamcybersafe.org/scholarships/raytheon-womens-scholarships/

Scholarships For Women Studying Information Security (SWSIS) Program Scholarship
Award amount: $5,000-$10,000
https://cra.org/cra-w/scholarships-and-awards/scholarships/swsis/

The Science, Mathematics and Research for Transformation (SMART) Scholarship for Service Program
Award amount: full tuition + salary + benefits
https://smartscholarshipprod.service-now.com/smart

Sourcefire Snort Scholarship
Award amount: $10,000
https://snort.org/community#snort_scholarship

The Stokes Program
Award amount: $30,000
https://www.intelligencecareers.gov/icstudents.html

Women In Computing Scholarship
Award amount: $1,000
https://www.loadview-testing.com/scholarship/

education: Support for Minorities and

You Won't Be Alone

Diversity in the cyber field is needed. Look for a mentor to lend you a hand.

White men predominate in cybersecurity as in STEM fields generally, but this is changing. Noel Kyle, Program Manager in Work Force Development at Homeland Security, observes that because cybersecurity is a complex and diverse issue, it follows that the work force must be complex and diverse. Rinki Sethi, Senior Director of Information Security at Palo Alto Networks, says that because cybersecurity teams need "thought diversity," hiring employees of different backgrounds and experiences just comes naturally.

Symantec, the international cybersecurity company that developed the Norton anti-virus software, has announced a commitment to improving the overall percentage of women and other underrepresented minorities in cybersecurity by 15% by 2020, with particular attention to increasing the percentage of women in executive leadership. Women currently make up only 11% of all cyber professionals. Symantec has set a goal of raising their overall percentage of women employed in cybersecurity by 15% by 2020.

Symantec partners with numerous professional and educational organizations and has developed the Symantec Cyber Career Connection to help prepare women and other underrepresented individuals for cyber careers. The DHS Office of Academic Engagement hosts free webinars for college and graduate students highlighting career paths and also internships available specifically for women and minorities.

Having mentors is a key component in school and career success. Schools and employers make mentoring a matter of planning, not luck. Rinki Sethi observes that cybersecurity is so broad that no one should give up interest or opt out because of weak skills at the introductory class level. Network to develop information about other aspects to cybersecurity. Don't hesitate to contact organizations and follow up on referrals.

NSA software development specialist Kate Plough emphasizes that mentors do not need to look like you in order to help with professional growth and development — four of her five mentors are men. Plough laughs about her middle school inspiration for a tech career in public service, the spy played by Jennifer Garner in the TV show "Alias," because she has ended up more like the white male tech-savvy sidekick played by Kevin Weisman. The lesson learned, she says, is to follow your interests. Above all, don't decide tech is not for you because you are in the minority. Keep developing your skills and look for support from the educators and professionals you meet — they are looking to support you.

careers: Companies of all Kinds

Help Wanted: Cyber Experts

From smoothies to satellites, there are many well-paying jobs in America's top companies for cyber sleuths.

Yes, the federal government is the largest employer of cybersecurity professionals. But many kinds of businesses rely on cybersecurity experts to protect their company's proprietary information and prevent hackers from holding data for ransom or stealing the personal information of clients and customers. Private-sector companies tend to pay higher salaries than government agencies, even to entry-level employees. Even better, skills and experience acquired in either public or private sector are attractive to both kinds of employers, so moving from government to the corporate world and vice versa is always an option.

Unless you're paying cash, every time you make a purchase, retailers and consumer services companies transmit your personally identifiable information, PII. PII includes everything that can be used standing alone or in combination to identify individuals and access bank accounts and credit cards. Protecting PII is the first obligation of companies that collect and store it — every online retailer, bank, utility, school, law firm, and medical facility! The simplest online purchase requires at least two exchanges of PII, and many transactions require more. Each exchange opens the door to identity theft. The Equifax hack of 2017 compromised the PII of nearly 150 million people.

But the world of valuable information extends beyond the individual. Consumer products companies have trade secrets to keep from competitors. Nike's newest shoes and the latest Apple iPhone are a big deal on Wall Street, not just on your street! Companies that engineer systems and new technology — to produce solar energy, for example, or run the local electricity grid, or send hazardous materials across the country — depend on protecting proprietary information to stay competitive and deliver promised services. Good cybersecurity is fundamental to good business.

It is no exaggeration to say that the right to privacy depends on cybersecurity experts working for retailers like Amazon and Walmart and producers like Sony and Apple. Increasingly, consumer goods are connected to the Internet, making them vulnerable to hackers. More sophisticated uses for artificial intelligence in our homes mean that more sophisticated cybersecurity technology will be needed to guard against more sophisticated hackers. Organized crime and foreign adversaries have an interest in consumer goods technology. Imagine a city held hostage through a device not all that different from the Amazon Echo!

Big Business
Top U. S. companies hiring cyber professionals

1. Apple
2. Federal Reserve Bank of New York
3. Patient First
4. Lockheed Martin
5. General Motors
6. Capital One
7. Cisco
8. Intel
9. Northrop Grumman
10. Boeing

SOURCE: INDEED

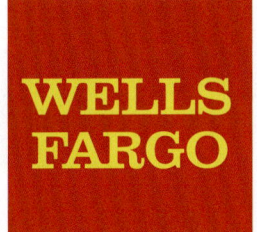

careers: Cybersecurity Companies

Palo Alto Networks' corporate office in California

Protection Is Their Mission

Companies that provide cybersecurity services to both government and industry can be a great career option.

Cybersecurity companies include corporations that are household names, such as IBM, and companies most of us have never heard of, like Seculore Solutions. These businesses provide cybersecurity expertise to government and private industry across a range of functions, from building technology structures to providing personnel for intelligence analysis and counterterrorism. They also have internal needs for information security. These options make for exciting careers.

Cybersecurity companies primarily engage in complex problem-solving in the design and protection of information systems. Every information system has to perform multiple functions. In information exchange, it is essential to protect the process and ensure verification of those who will access the information. In information storage, it is vital to keep unauthorized users out. Every day, codes and programs for tricking, penetrating, and disabling all kinds of cyber systems are being developed all over the world.

Complex problem-solving demands having teams of professionals with a wide range of skills and backgrounds. Palo Alto Networks in California is among the foremost cybersecurity companies. Senior Director of Information Security Rinki Sethi says that cybersecurity is the broadest field she knows because any degree can be the basis for a career. Cybersecurity teams include law-

IBM Security Headquarters in Cambridge, MA

Symantec headquarters in Mountain View, CA

yers because navigating legal and policy issues is part of strategic planning. Having executives with expertise in project management is as important as having "white-hat hackers" who simulate attacks and develop defenses.

Also needed are people with communication skills who like to interact with clients — and engage in outreach to boost education and training so that people like you make cybersecurity their career goal.

Sethi laughs when she describes cybersecurity as a career for anyone who dislikes boredom. She, like other cybersecurity company professionals, is on the frontier of development and sees how what she and her team do affects information security. What she loves about her job is that she is making an impact for good on the world. "Every day," she says," I feel aware of the connection between what I am doing and the world at large."

Besides the joy she takes sharing her own love for her career in information security, Sethi takes seriously the high demand for cyber professionals and is active in work force development. She and her team participate in collegiate cyber defense competitions. She also was engaged in Palo Alto Networks' 2017 initiative with the Girl Scouts of America to create 18 cyber badges, based on cyber education from middle school through high school, which will be available to any scout starting in fall 2018. Also involved in the GSA project, Davina Pruitt-Mentle, Lead Academic for Engagement at NICE, says that the goal is coming up with fun activities to boost kids' tech and thinking skills in K-12. Palo Alto employees structured the badges, built the curriculum, and have trained troop leaders. Having opportunities to enable anyone to gain skills and experience for pursuing a career in cyber is a big plus for Sethi.

Requirements for employment with cybersecurity companies are often but not always the same as those for government agencies. This is because in addition to working on projects related to national defense and law enforcement, employees of cybersecurity companies sometimes work at restricted-access government sites. Keep in mind, however, that because cybersecurity companies serve other clients and have other priorities, you nevertheless can be eligible for employment at a cybersecurity company even if you are not eligible for security clearances.

careers: Work for the Government

Your Country Needs You

With cyber attacks on the rise, protecting and defending in cyberspace is mission-critical.

The federal government currently is the largest employer of cybersecurity professionals. National defense is an obvious reason why. What sets government apart from private industry is mission, not skill sets. Military and civilian cybersecurity experts work in intelligence analysis, counter-intelligence, counter-terrorism, and support to special operations. Government careers are also in law enforcement, tracking national and global developments in financial crime, human trafficking, extremist organizations, and more, in order to prevent crime and punish criminals. State and local government law enforcement agencies also employ cybersecurity professionals.

In addition, every government agency manages its own information and records system, and the federal government oversees large repositories of information. Since 9/11, many agencies have been mandated to share information or collaborate in multi-agency task forces. Exchanged information ranges from PII (personally identifiable information) to top-secret intelligence, and it all needs to be kept safe from hack-

careers: Work for the Government

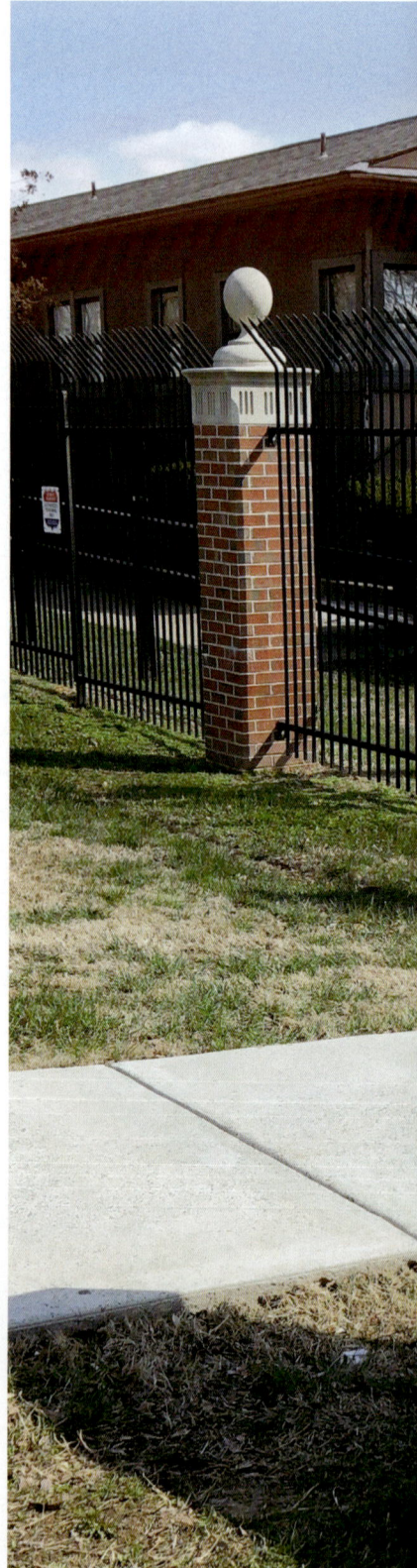

ing as well as accidental spills to those without the "need to know." Just as in the private sector, some government careers require using communication and management skills more than hands-on computing skills. Law comes into play because of agency regulations and even the Constitution — we are protected against unreasonable search and seizure and have rights to due process. The anticipated national deficit of cyber employees for jobs is approaching two million, so many federal agencies are aggressively promoting work force development and education. Because these government jobs require a security clearance, applicants must be both U.S. citizens and clearance-eligible.

Kate Plough, Software Development Specialist at the NSA, was a Stokes Scholar with a four-year scholarship and summer internships that cemented her love of computer science in a government career. She observes that, in addition to working on interesting problems that arise only in government, "I know that people use what I do, that what I do is needed and makes a positive difference in the world." She also has opportunities to shift gears, develop new skills, and move within her agency. Equally important to her is that mentoring and outreach are part of her job, giving her a chance to "pay forward what I had" by mentoring current Stokes Scholarship recipients and participating in the NSA's Cybersecurity Camps. She is proud of the NSA's Day of Cyber, an online interactive experience of a day in the life of six NSA cybersecurity professionals that's free to anyone anywhere in the U.S.

Plough's work entails using computers to systematize problem-solving, creating programs to solve a particular problem whenever it arises. She says she gets into the mind-set of large-scale problem-solving by using computer science to solve the word games and math problems that turn up in the NSA's "Daily Puzzle." While she appreciates that her experience is transferable to the private sector, she loves combining problem-solving with public service and enjoys the camaraderie of working among others with the same sense of mission in national security.

Program Manager Noel Kyle and IT Specialist Princess Young of DHS share Kate's enthusiasm for cybersecurity careers in public service. For those who understand the science and enjoy using communication skills, one of the best opportunities in government, says Princess, is promoting interest in cybersecurity careers to ensure that there is a work force to meet future need. Both Noel and Princess enjoy opportunities to travel and meet many different kinds of people.

Young engages in outreach and develops teacher-training programs so that schools anywhere in the U.S. can support cybersecurity education and extracurricular activities. DHS works with non-profits, like the Girl Scouts, to make sure opportunities to get the skills and education for cyber careers are available to everyone. Noel Kyle describes work force development as building a pipeline for people, many of whom will become first responders in cybersecurity. It's a big pipeline! Considering that 22 separate agencies are within DHS, it is no surprise that both Young and Kyle find their work to be fast-paced, with challenges to stay current with global, national, and agency developments in cyber threats and cybersecurity.

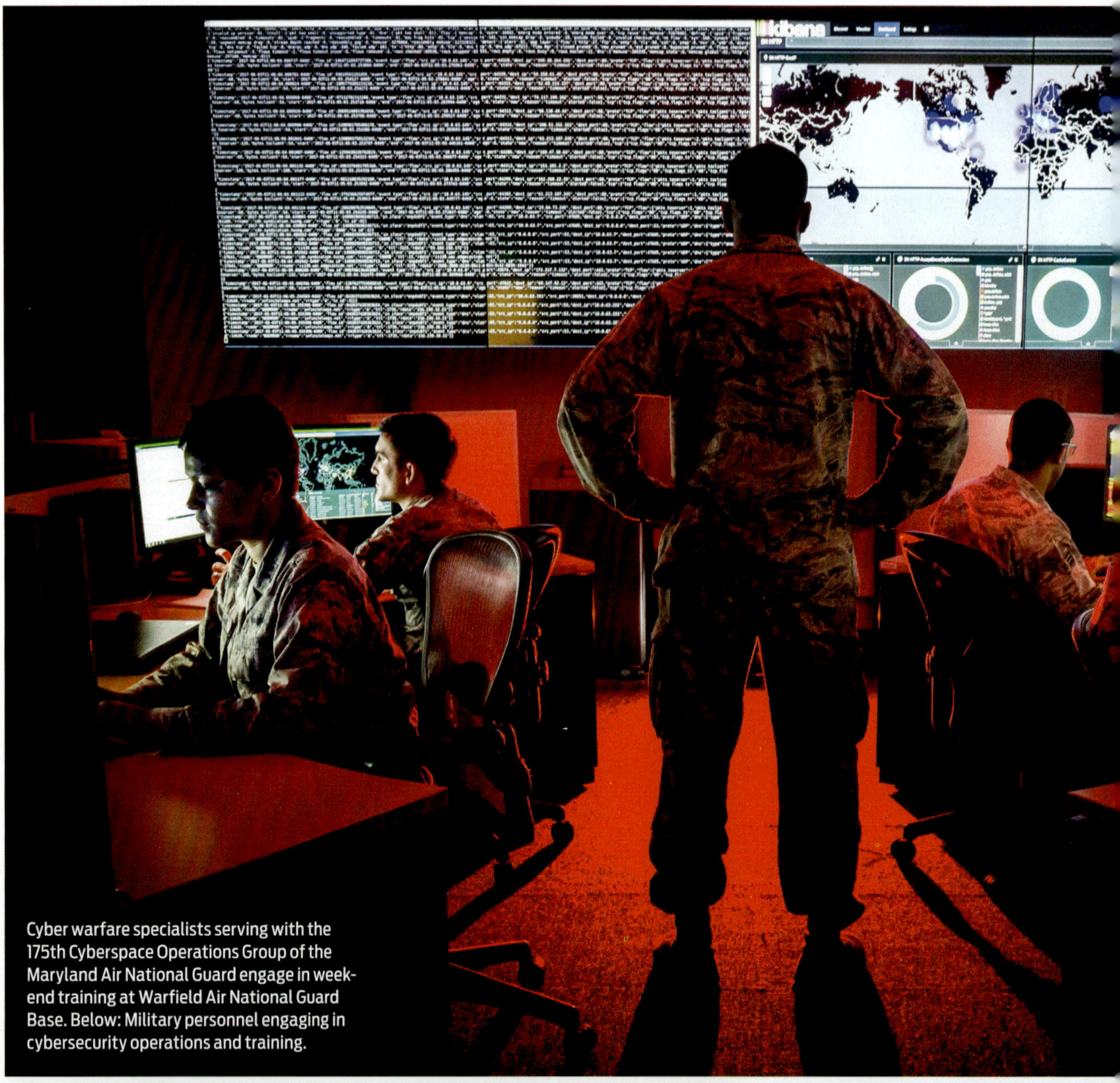

careers: Military

Cyber warfare specialists serving with the 175th Cyberspace Operations Group of the Maryland Air National Guard engage in weekend training at Warfield Air National Guard Base. Below: Military personnel engaging in cybersecurity operations and training.

Enlist in Your Future

"Cyberspace is not just a computer on your desktop. It's the way that we as an Air Force intend to fly and fight," General Robert J. Elder, Jr., USAF

Our nation's military is all volunteer, equally open to young women and men. If you are oriented to public service and know that college is not yet for you for either financial or academic reasons, laying the groundwork for both cybersecurity education and career by enlisting in the military after high school is worth looking into.

Apart from the U.S. Cyber Command, the Army, Navy, Marines, and Air Force each have cyber commands, and there are literally over 100 specialized functions, teams, and joint operations working in combat and support in cyber-related assignments.

It's wise to get basic certifications in cybersecurity before enlisting. Military assignments are just that, assignments, and they are based on aptitude tests each branch of the service uses to determine where to place you. But you can request specific commands and also use free time to develop computer skills and cyber certifications to qualify for the cyber-related commands that interest you. And get this: the military offers training and will pay for training, including in foreign languages, which, when combined with tech skills, makes for a very strong basis for a cybersecurity career. Stay in the military and continue on to higher education, becoming an officer, or leave the service and use veterans' benefits to fund your own cyber degree program!

The different branches of the military have different missions and different requirements. They station personnel in different parts of the country and the world. If you have no preference, study up on the purpose of each branch, what jobs are on offer and where. Don't overlook the Coast Guard. Alternatively, you can enlist in the reserves or the National Guard. While joining either of these is not the same as joining a service branch for active duty, both offer salary, education benefits, and help with career development and obtaining a security clearance, just as active duty service does.

facts and figures

PAYING OFF
Cybersecurity salaries in the U.S.

Job Title	Median Annual Salary
Security Consultant	$123,885
IT Security Specialist	$109,366
Network Security Engineer	$107,931
Information Security Analyst	$92,600
Security Analyst	$85,238
Security Engineer	$81,036
Intelligence Analyst	$51,605
Information Technology Specialist	$41,579

SOURCE: INDEED. SALARY DATA COMES FROM 368,033 DATA POINTS COLLECTED DIRECTLY FROM EMPLOYEES, USERS, AND PAST AND PRESENT JOB ADVERTISEMENT ON INDEED OVER THE LAST 12 MONTHS.

FAST GROWING & WELL PAID

Jobs for cybersecurity analysts are expected to grow by **28%** between now and 2026, with a median annual salary of **$92,600**.

SOURCE: US DEPARTMENT OF LABOR, BUREAU OF LABOR STATISTICS